THE
Chocolate
Lover's
COOKBOOK

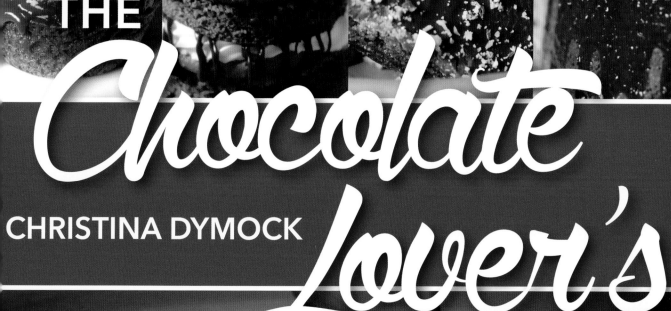

THE

Chocolate

CHRISTINA DYMOCK

Lover's

COOKBOOK

From the author of *One Dirty Bowl* and *The Healthy Family Slow Cooker*

FRONT TABLE BOOKS | AN IMPRINT OF CEDAR FORT, INC. | SPRINGVILLE, UTAH

ISBN 13: 978-1-4621-1723-9

Published by Front Table Books, an imprint of Cedar Fort, Inc.
2373 W. 700 S., Springville, UT 84663
Distributed by Cedar Fort, Inc., www.cedarfort.com

LIBRARY OF CONGRESS CATALOGING-IN-PUBLICATION DATA

Dymock, Christina, 1978- author.
The chocolate lover's cookbook / Christina Dymock.
     pages cm
Includes index.
ISBN 978-1-4621-1723-9 (layflat binding : acid-free paper)
1. Desserts. 2. Cooking (Chocolate) I. Title.
TX773.D8648 2015
641.6'374--dc23

2015028093

Cover design by M. Shaun McMurdie
Page design by M. Shaun McMurdie and Michelle May
Cover design © 2015 by Lyle Mortimer
Edited by Justin Greer

Printed in China

10 9 8 7 6 5 4 3 2 1

Printed on acid-free paper

For Grandma Lucy

and Grandma Joyce

61

103

18

29

108

Table of Contents

introduction *ix*

chocolate info *1*

brownies and bars *7*

cakes and pies *31*

cookies *55*

desserts *79*

candy *101*

sauces, fillings, and frostings *119*

index *136*

measurement equivalents *133*

about the author *134*

Introduction

Hello, Fellow Chocolate Lovers,

If you're like me, you've been a chocolate lover for as long as you can remember. I don't have any recollection of my first taste of chocolate. It's probably buried as deep as the memory of my first pair of shoes or my first laugh. The love runs deep.

It wasn't until I began to assemble recipes for this book that I realized chocolate was expertly woven into my childhood by those who loved me most. You'll find several recipes in this book from my mom. She is a connoisseur and can wield a bag of chocolate chips with skill. Likewise, both my maternal and paternal grandmothers have contributed recipes that were mainstays as I was growing up. I looked forward to finding these treasures at family dinners and holiday parties. When I bake with my children, I like to tell them who the recipe came from. Not only am I sharing a time-tested recipe, teaching kitchen skills, and getting in quality time, I'm sharing part of their heritage. If you're a chocolate lover, you pass that love on to those you cherish without ever planning it out. It's in your DNA, like blue eyes and cowlicks.

Chocolate lovers span the globe. It doesn't matter which country you are in, you can always find chocolate. Some areas of the world like their chocolate bitter, while others like it sweet. But we unite together in our desire for cocoa. We give chocolate, we hide chocolate, we devour chocolate, we savor chocolate, and we break off tastes for toddlers, delighting in the way their eyes light up.

What I worked toward as I selected, measured, stirred, dumped, and melted chocolate were recipes that would not only tempt chocolate lovers, but become part of your family culture.

From one chocolate lover to another, I hope you enjoy!

Chocolate Info

There are great tomes full of information about where chocolate comes from, the history behind the bean, and the magical transformation from bean to chocolate bar. If you're a chocolate lover, you probably already have a working knowledge of the history of chocolate. What I want to provide here are tips in working with chocolate that can help you in the kitchen.

Tasting Chocolate

Chocolate is an experience. It's not just the flavor, it's the sight, smell, taste, and even sound of chocolate that makes savoring your favorite treats so pleasurable.

In order to get the full experience out of a piece of chocolate, you'll first want to break it in half and inhale the aroma. Go ahead and lift the chocolate right up to your nose and take a deep breath in. What do you smell? The cocoa? Of course, but what else? Can you smell berries, mushrooms, pine, grapefruit, or hazelnuts? The DNA of the cocoa bean will determine the sub flavors in chocolate.

Once you have deeply inhaled the smell of the chocolate, rub the piece between your thumb and finger. But it will melt! Yes, that's what you want it to do. You want to feel the texture of the chocolate on your skin. Milk chocolates will be smooth and melt easily while dark chocolates can feel rough. Take a moment to inhale the aroma once again and see if you note any changes that melting the chocolate has brought out. Finally, place the chocolate on your tongue and hold it to the roof of your mouth. Leave it there for a count of 15. It's torture! Being so close to the prize and not allowed to consume it yet. Finally, chew the chocolate being sure to cover the different areas of your tongue. When you swallow, take in a breath through your mouth and you may be surprised at the lingering taste you only glimpsed when breathing in the chocolate scent.

Go ahead and give this method a try. Try it on your first bite of every chocolate bar, chocolate chip, and chocolate chunk. After you've discovered the true taste of the chocolate, feel free to gobble up the rest.

Chopping Chocolate

Chopping chocolate is as close to a chore as working with chocolate will ever be. The large blocks of chocolate, sometimes weighing 10 pounds or more, can be difficult to manage in the home kitchen. However, dipping chocolates requires vast amounts of chocolate and the chore must be accomplished.

Chopping Block

Use a wood breadboard or chopping block. If possible, dedicate this board to chopping chocolate so you don't feel bad when you leave gouges. Keeping the chopping block for chocolate only also decreases the chances of it absorbing bacteria from other foods. Your chocolate experience should be purely chocolate; not chocolate mixed with broccoli.

Freezer Paper

Place a piece of freezer paper or parchment paper on your cutting board. When you're done chopping, you can lift two sides of the paper and funnel the small pieces and shavings into your melting pot.

The Right Knife

Use a large chef's knife. Don't try to use a butter knife or steak knife to cut chocolate. Go with the largest knife you own and be sure to take precautions to protect your precious fingers—you only get ten.

Cut Corners

Instead of trying to cut along the flat side of a piece of chocolate, cut at the corners. When the corner becomes too flat, twist the chocolate and cut on another. Repeat as needed until done.

Food Processor

It is possible to chop chocolate in a food processor. However, chocolate is probably the toughest thing you will ever put across the blade. It will tax the motor and dull a cheap blade. Therefore, if you don't have a high-quality machine, do not attempt this technique.

Chop the chocolate into pieces that will fit down the feed tube. Fit the coarse grating disk into the processor and pulse to chop the chocolate.

Melting Chocolate

There are several different methods for melting chocolate and you may have your favorite. However, some recipes specify the way the chocolate should be melted. Always follow the recipe and if it doesn't specify, you can use your preferred method.

Double Broiler

This is my go-to method for melting fine chocolate as I have better control over the temperature of the chocolate than I would when using the microwave or stovetop.

Fill a pan with 1–2 inches of water and place it on the burner. Set the heat to medium-low. Once the water starts to steam, turn the temperature down to low. Set a glass bowl on top of the pan. The bowl should not touch the water. Add the chocolate to the bowl and stir occasionally, increasing the frequency until smooth. Remove from the heat and use according to recipe directions.

Frying Pan

I first learned this method as an apprentice in my family's chocolate adventures. The advantage to this method is that your chocolate is portable. You can set up on the table and spread out to do your chocolate project.

Fill an electric frying pan with 1–2 inches of water. Turn the frying pan on to the lowest heat setting and allow it to warm up for 5 minutes. You should be able to place your fingers in the water and it should feel just barely warmer than your skin never warm and never cold. Place a heavy-duty pan in the water and then put the chocolate in the pan. Continue to monitor the water. You cannot turn the temperature up on the frying pan to try to speed things along. This is a slow process. It can take up to an hour to melt a pan of chocolate this way; however, the slow process is worth it when the hand-dipped chocolates turn out perfect.

Microwave

Place the chocolate in a microwave safe bowl. Cook the chocolate for 1 minute at half power. Stir. The chocolate may not have melted much at this point, but it's important that you cut the cook time down to 30 seconds at half power from here on out. Repeat the process, stirring between cook times to distribute the heat and eliminate hot spots that could burn. Once the chocolate is smooth, use according to recipe directions.

Stovetop

If you're melting chocolate chips or other chocolate that has a high wax content, you can melt them directly on the stove top. Simply pour the chips into a saucepan and turn the stove on to low. Stir constantly. When there are only a few bumps left, remove the pan from the burner and continue to stir until smooth.

Chocolate Equivalents

There's nothing that can replace chocolate. However, when a recipe calls for 2 ounces of unsweetened chocolate, and you don't have any on-hand, you can substitute cocoa powder and oil in the recipe. There's other great information here. I hope it comes in handy.

Types of Chocolate

There are many different types of chocolate on the market. Each type has its place in baking. Some can be interchanged while others just can't be replaced. For example, if a chocolate chip cookie recipe calls for milk chocolate chips, you'd be okay substituting semi-sweet chocolate chips. However, if a recipe called for ⅓ cup cocoa powder, you couldn't use ⅓ cup semi-sweet chocolate chips. As you read about the different types of chocolate listed below, you'll see that they have different structures, ingredients, and cocoa potency.

UNSWEETENED CHOCOLATE—Those baking bars you find in the chocolate baking section do not contain sweeteners, like sugar, hence the name. They start out as chocolate liquid that is poured into molds to make bars. You wouldn't want to eat this chocolate on its own as it has a very bitter flavor. It is 100% cocoa.

DARK CHOCOLATE—This chocolate usually contains at least 50% cacao though it can contain up to 80% depending on the manufacturer. Dark chocolate does not contain milk or cream. You can use dark chocolate for baking an while you can eat it on its own, it may still taste bitter.

SEMI-SWEET CHOCOLATE—In order to qualify as semi-sweet, chocolate must contain at least 35% cacao. As with dark chocolate, semi-sweet chocolate does not contain milk or cream. It also has 50% more cacao than it has sugar.

MILK CHOCOLATE—As the name states, this chocolate will be mixed with milk products. You can see the difference in the color. Dark chocolates can be almost black while milk chocolates are a light brown. Milk chocolate must have at least 10% cacao. Milk chocolate is one of the sweetest chocolates.

1 cup chocolate chips	6 ounces of chocolate
2 cups of chocolate chips	1 (12-oz.) bag of chocolate chips
3 tablespoons semi-sweet chocolate chips	1 ounce semi-sweet baking chocolate
1 ounce unsweetened chocolate + 1 tablespoon sugar	1 ounce chocolate chips
3 tablespoons + 1 tablespoon shortening	1 ounce unsweetened chocolate (bar form)

Blooming Chocolate

As wonderful as chocolate is, it isn't indestructible. If chocolate is heated too quickly or cooled too fast, it will bloom. Blooming is when the cocoa butter separates on a molecular level from the cacao. A white blush on chocolate chips is not a reason to throw them out, you can still use them for baking; however, you will not be able to use them as a dip for candies. If you see the same bloom on your dipping chocolate, it has spoiled and must be released into the wild. To prevent this from happening, store your chocolate in an airtight container in a cool dry place.

Brownies and Bars

9   brownie tips & definitions

10   fudgety-fudge brownies

13   nothin' but chocolate gooey bars

14   snowball brownies

17   pecan and chocolate cookie bars

18   cookie dough brownies

21   the king of brownies

22   grandma joyce's 24-hour brownies

25   mint brownies

26   striped brownies

29   pumpkin cheesecake & chocolate swirl brownies

Brownie tips

Do you tend to overcook your brownies? If you do, the edges will become hard and the center will be tough. Here are a few hints to help you bake the perfect brownie.

Cook Time

Always set your timer for the lowest cook time listed. The reason a range of cook times is given, is that all ovens cook at different speeds and the pan you use can make a big difference. Metal pans tend to cook faster than glass pans. Check the brownies at the lowest cook time and add a few minutes if needed.

Sight

If the batter jiggles when you move the pan, the brownies are not done. Also, if the edges start to pull away from the pan, it means the brownies have been overcooked.

Touch

If you press lightly in the center of the brownies, they should feel set. If they do not, they will need extra cooking time. Be careful not to burn yourself when using this technique. A much safer test is the toothpick test.

Toothpick Test

Insert a wooden toothpick in the center of the brownies. If it comes out covered in wet batter, the brownies will need more time. If the toothpick comes out with crumbs, the brownie is ready. If the toothpick comes out clean, the brownie is overcooked and will be hard around the edges.

Definitions

Fudgy Brownie (fʌdʒi bɹaʊni)

A piece of heaven with a dense, moist, chocolate intensity somewhere between eating a chocolate torte and a truffle. The batter will be dense.

Chewy Brownie (tʃui bɹaʊni)

A moist morsel of perfection, a chewy brownie will use more flour than a fudge brownie, whole eggs, and lots of butter. The batter will be thick and spread easily.

Cakey Brownie (keɪki bɹaʊni)

A specimen of spectacular essence. To make a cakey brownie, you must beat the butter and sugar(s) together as if baking a cake. The recipe may also include milk to keep the batter moist and baking powder to leaven the brownie. The batter will be thin and pour easily.

fudgety-fudge brownies

A dense fudge brownie with frosting. You can't beat these brownies for being pretty. They cut beautifully with few crumbs and will hold their shape. If you want a brownie to present on a plate, this one does a terrific job.

serves 48
Ingredients

2 cups butter, melted

1 cups sugar

1 cup brown sugar

2 eggs

¼ cup milk

2 tsp. vanilla

1½ cup flour

¾ cup cocoa powder

½ cup chopped walnuts for topping, optional

1 batch Fudge Frosting (recipe on page 124)

Directions

Preheat the oven to 350 degrees. Line a jelly roll pan with aluminum foil and spray with nonstick cooking spray. Set aside.

In a large mixing bowl, combine the butter, sugar, and brown sugar. Add the eggs, milk and vanilla and mix well. Mix in the flour and cocoa powder stirring until the dry ingredients are incorporated well. Spread into the prepared pan and bake for 16-20 minutes or until a toothpick inserted in the center comes out clean. Frost with Fudge Frosting and top with nuts if desired.

nothin' but chocolate gooey bars

Sometimes you just need a dose of chocolate. And then sometimes, you need an overdose of chocolate. These gooey bars will fix any chocolate need.

serves 12

Ingredients

1 cup flour
1 cup sugar
½ cup cocoa
½ Tbsp. soda
½ tsp. salt

1 tsp. vanilla
1 egg
½ cup canola oil
1 cup milk chocolate chips
½ cup semi-sweet chocolate chips

½ cup white chocolate chips
½ cup special dark chocolate fudge ice cream topping
1 (14-oz.) can sweetened condensed milk

Directions

Preheat the oven to 350 degrees. Spray a 9 × 13 inch pan with nonstick cooking spray and set aside.

In a large mixing bowl, combine the flour, sugar, cocoa, soda, salt, vanilla, egg, and oil. Reserve 1 cup of the mixture and pour the rest into the prepared pan. Bake for 10-12 minutes or until set. Immediately spread the milk, semi-sweet, and white chocolate chips over the crust. Set aside. In a small mixing bowl, combine the ice cream topping and sweetened condensed milk until smooth. Pour over the chocolate chips and cook for 20-22 minutes. Allow bars to cool completely before cutting.

snowball brownies

Our new family favorite. Since developing this recipe, I've been asked to make it once a week. If you love the combination of marshmallow and chocolate, this is your brownie. These brownies have a cake-like consistency Stuffed with Marshmallow Filling (recipe on page 120), frosted with a marshmallow buttercream frosting, and sprinkled with shredded coconut. They're rich, so plan accordingly.

serves 16

Brownie

1 batch Marshmallow Filling recipe on page 120	½ cup cocoa powder	1 tsp. baking powder
¾ cup butter, melted	1 tsp. vanilla	¼ tsp. baking soda
1¼ cup sugar	2 eggs	1 cup milk
	1 ½ cups flour	

Frosting

1 cup plus 1 tsp. butter, at room temperature, divided	2 tsp. vanilla	¼ tsp. salt
	2 cups powdered sugar	2 cups mini marshmallows

Coconut Garnish

2 cups shredded coconut	1 Tbsp. cornstarch	1 drop food coloring

For the brownies

Preheat the oven to 350 degrees. Spray a 9 × 13 inch pan with nonstick cooking spray and set aside.

In a medium-sized mixing bowl, stir together the melted butter, sugar, cocoa powder, and vanilla. Add the eggs and mix until just combined. Add the flour, baking powder, baking soda, and milk and mix until well combined scraping down the sides of the bowl as necessary. Pour the brownie batter into the prepared pan and cook for 25–30 minutes or until a toothpick inserted in the center comes out clean. Allow the brownies to cool to room temperature.

Fill a pastry bag with the marshmallow filling and add a 2A tip. Insert the tip into the brownies and squeeze the marshmallow filling into the brownies making holes 1 inch apart.

For the frosting

In a medium-sized mixing bowl, whip together 1 cup of butter, vanilla, powdered sugar and salt. Set aside. In a medium-sized saucepan, melt the marshmallows and 1 teaspoon butter over medium-low heat stirring occasionally. Once melted, add the marshmallow to the frosting and beat until light and fluffy. Frost the brownies.

For the coconut garnish

Place the coconut, cornstarch, and food coloring in the blender. Pulse until the color is evenly distributed and the coconut is in smaller pieces. Sprinkle the coconut over the top of the freshly frosted brownies. Cut the brownies and serve.

pecan and chocolate cookie bars

These super sweet cookies have all the benefits of a chocolate pecan pie without having to make a pie crust.

serves 16

Ingredients

26 graham crackers, divided

1 cup sugar

½ cup milk

½ cup butter plus 3 Tbsp., divided

1 egg

2 tsp. vanilla, divided

¼ tsp. salt

½ cup pecans, chopped

1 cup flaked coconut

½ cup brown sugar

1½ cups semi-sweet chocolate chips

¼ cup water

2 cups powdered sugar

Directions

Line a 9 × 13 inch pan with aluminum foil. Place 7 graham crackers across the bottom of the pan; set aside. Crush 12 of the graham crackers and set aside. Reserve the remaining graham crackers.

In a medium-sized saucepan, stir together the sugar, milk, ½ cup butter. Beat the egg in a separate bowl and then add it to the pan. Bring the mixture to a boil over medium heat.

Remove from stove top and add the crushed graham crackers, pecans, and coconut. Stir together and allow to cool for 10 minutes and then spread the mixture over the crackers in the pan. Top with the remaining crackers.

In a small saucepan, bring to a boil the brown sugar, chocolate chips, and water over medium heat. Remove the pan from the stovetop and add 1 teaspoon vanilla, 3 tablespoons of butter, and the powdered sugar. Beat together until the mixture is smooth.

Spread the chocolate sauce over the top of the graham crackers. Cover the pan and refrigerate overnight. Store in the refrigerator.

cookie dough brownies

Deciding where to put these scrumptious bars was a conundrum. Do I put them in the cookie section because of the cookie dough topping or do they go in the brownie section because of the brownie bottom. Since they are a cut-to-serve dessert, they ended up here. But, they will certainly satisfy your craving for either cookies or brownies. Feel free to share liberally!

For Brownie Layer

½ cup butter at room temperature

1 cup sugar

3 eggs

1 teaspoon vanilla

1 ¼ cup flour

1/3 cup cocoa

¼ teaspoon baking soda

For Cookie Dough Layer

½ cup butter at room temperature

¼ cup sugar

½ cup brown sugar

3 tablespoons cream

1 teaspoon vanilla

1 cup flour

1 cup mini chocolate chips

For Topping

1 batch of One Bag Ganache (page 121)

Directions

Preheat the oven to 350 degrees. Spray a 9x13 inch pan with nonstick cooking spray and set aside.

For Brownie Layer

In a medium-sized mixing bowl, cream together the butter and sugar. Add the eggs and vanilla and mix well. Mix in the flour, cocoa, and baking soda. Spread batter into the prepared pan and bake for 16-20 minutes or until a toothpick inserted in the center comes out clean or with a few crumbs. Remove from oven and place in the fridge for 1 hour to cool or place on a wire rack for 2 hours before adding the cookie layer.

For Cookie Layer

In a medium-sized mixing bowl, cream the butter, sugar and brown sugar until light and fluffy. Add the cream and vanilla and mix well. Incorporate the flour a quarter-cup at a time and then fold in the chocolate chips. Spread over cooled brownies. Top with the ganache and allow to set before serving. Store brownies in the refrigerator.

the king of brownies

serves 20

Ingredients

1½ cups miniature
marshmallows

3 Tbsp. creamy peanut butter

3 Tbsp. heavy cream

1½ cup sugar

¾ cup butter

¼ cup cocoa powder

1½ cups flour

¾ cups quick-oats

1 tsp. salt

1 tsp. vanilla

1 egg

Directions

Preheat the oven to 350 degrees. Line a 9 × 13 inch pan with aluminum foil and spray with nonstick cooking spray. Set aside.

In a medium-sized saucepan, melt the marshmallows, peanut butter, and heavy cream over medium heat. Stir frequently. Once the marshmallows have melted and the mixture is smooth, add the sugar and butter. Stir until the butter melts. Remove the pan from the heat and add the cocoa powder, flour, oats, salt, vanilla, and egg. Mix well. Pour batter into prepared pan and spread to the edges. Bake for 20–25 minutes or until a toothpick inserted in the center comes out clean. Allow to cool before frosting (page 124).

grandma joyce's
24-hour brownies

If my Grandma Joyce had a specialty dessert, it was these brownies!
They've been requested for birthdays, church socials, bake sales, family
dinners, and neighborhood get-togethers. It is important to use regular-sized
marshmallows cut in half and not miniature marshmallows. They are called
24-hour brownies because they can be made 24 hours in advance, which
is advantageous if you're planning a party or have a busy schedule. They
also take several hours to set, so plan accordingly.

serves 16

Ingredients

1 (10-oz.) bag regular-sized
marshmallows

1 cup butter, melted

⅓ cup cocoa

2 cups sugar

4 eggs

2 tsp. vanilla

1½ cups flour

½ tsp. salt

2 cups roughly chopped
walnuts, divided (optional)

Fudge Frosting (recipe on
page 124)

Directions

Using kitchen shears, cut the marshmallows in half and place them in a bowl; set aside.

Preheat the oven to 350 degrees. Line a 10½ × 15½-inch jelly roll pan with aluminum foil and
spray with nonstick cooking spray. Set aside.

In a large mixing bowl, combine the butter, cocoa, and sugar. Add the eggs one at a time beating
well between additions. Add the vanilla, flour, and salt. Mix well. If desired, add 1 ½ cups walnuts
to the batter. Pour into prepared pan and bake for 25 minutes or until a toothpick inserted in
the center comes out clean. Remove from oven. Carefully line the marshmallows, cut side down,
across the brownies. Small spaces between marshmallows is okay as the marshmallows will
grow as they cook. Return the pan to the oven and cook for 5 minutes or until the marshmallows
double in size but do not brown. Remove the pan from the oven and allow the brownies to cool
before frosting with Fudge Frosting (page 124) and sprinkling with the remaining half cup of
walnuts. Allow to set for 4 hours or cover and allow to set overnight before cutting.

mint brownies

These are the brownies that people snitch. They whittle away at them, enjoying every stolen morsel. If you'd like to change things up, try replacing the mint flavoring with lemon, orange, or even cherry flavoring. Once you try one type, you'll want to try them all.

serves 24

Ingredients

1 batch of One-Bag Chocolate Ganache (recipe on page 121)

Brownie

1 cup butter, melted	1 tsp. vanilla	⅔ cup cocoa
2 cups sugar	2 cups flour	½ tsp. salt
4 eggs		

Mint Topping

1 cup sugar	½ cup butter	1 tsp. mint flavoring
½ tsp. salt	1 tsp. vanilla	3 drops green food coloring
1 cup cream		

Directions

Preheat the oven to 350 degrees. Line a 9 × 13-inch pan with aluminum foil and spray with nonstick cooking spray. Set aside.

For the brownies

Mix the butter and sugar together until just combined. Add the eggs and vanilla, stir well. Add the flour, cocoa, and salt. Mix until just combined, scraping down the sides of the bowl as necessary. Spread batter in the prepared pan and bake for 28–35 minutes or until a toothpick inserted in the center comes out clean. Allow to cool before topping.

For the mint topping

Blend the sugar, salt, and cream in a medium-sized saucepan. Add the butter and cook over medium-low heat. Cook until the butter melts; stir occasionally. Once the butter melts, bring the mixture to a boil and simmer for 20 minutes. Remove from heat and allow to cool. Stir in the vanilla and mint flavorings and the green food coloring. Spread over cooled brownies. Top with a fresh batch of One-Bag Chocolate Ganache. Allow the ganache to set before cutting the brownies.

striped brownies

Covered in chocolate glaze, these brownies are a little extra work with a huge payoff.

serves 36

Ingredients

3¼ cups flour	⅓ cup cocoa	3 sticks butter, divided
2 tsp. baking powder	1½ cups semi-sweet chocolate chips	2 tsp. vanilla
1 tsp. salt		4 eggs

Glaze

1 (12-oz.) package milk chocolate chips	2 Tbsp. butter	white chocolate candy melts
	1½ cups cream	

Directions

Preheat the oven to 350 degrees. Line a jelly roll pan with aluminum foil and spray with nonstick cooking spray. Set aside.

In a large mixing bowl, whisk together the flour, baking powder, salt, and cocoa. Set aside.

Melt 1 tablespoon butter and chocolate chips over low heat. Once the chocolate is smooth, remove the pan from the heat and add the vanilla and eggs. Slowly add the chocolate mixture to the flour mixture. Spread the batter in the prepared pan. Don't spread all the way to the edges. Bake for 40-45 minutes or until a toothpick inserted in the center comes out clean. Allow to cool completely.

Line a cookie sheet with parchment paper and place a wire rack on top.

Remove the brownies from the pan by lifting the foil lining out. Cut the edges off and cut the brownies into 36 pieces. Place the on the wire rack.

For the glaze

Melt the chocolate chips, butter, and cream over low heat until the mixture is smooth. Spoon the glaze over the brownies.

Follow the package direction to melt the white chocolate candy melts. Use a plastic bag with a small hole cut in the corner to drizzle the chocolate over the brownie squares. Let the glaze set before serving.

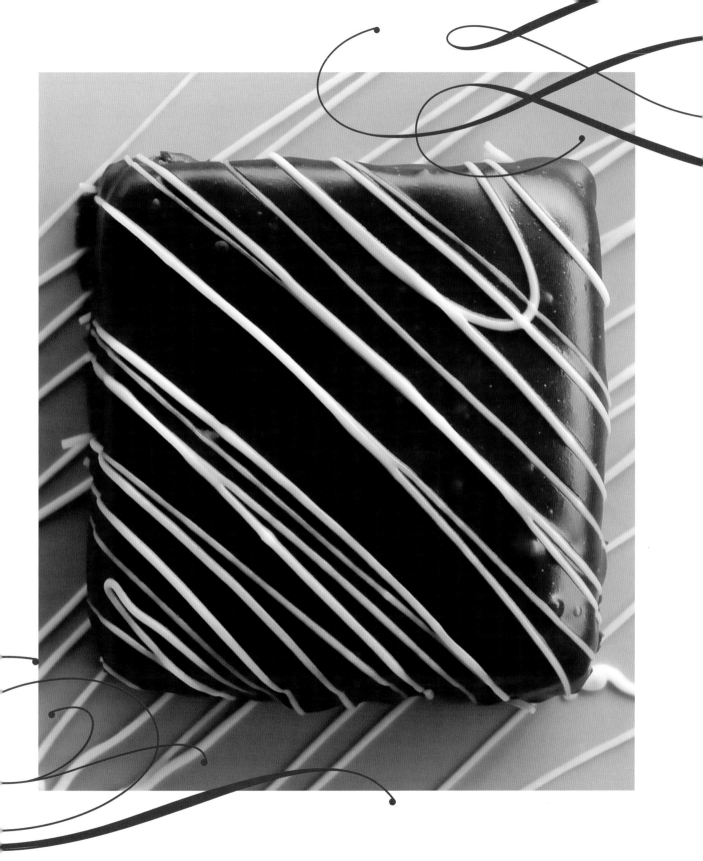

pumpkin cheesecake & chocolate swirl brownies

Decadent. Rich. Voluptuous.

Serves 12

For Brownies

1 cup dark chocolate chips	2 eggs	¾ cup flour
½ cup butter	1 teaspoon vanilla	
¾ cup sugar	½ teaspoon salt	

For the Pumpkin Cheesecake

4 ounces cream cheese at room temperature	1 egg	A pinch of cloves
½ cup pumpkin puree	¼ cup sugar	A pinch of ginger
	1 teaspoon cinnamon	

Directions

Preheat the oven to 350 degrees. Spray an 8x8-inch pan with nonstick cooking spray and set aside.

Cut the butter into 16 sections. Place the pieces in a small saucepan and add the chocolate. Melt over medium-low heat until smooth, stir occasionally. When the chocolate is done, remove it from the heat and allow it to cool while you stir the sugar, eggs, vanilla, salt, and flour together in a medium-sized mixing bowl. Once you can touch the bottom of the chocolate pan and it's just warm to the touch, add the chocolate to the brownie batter and stir well. Pour half the brownie mixture into the prepared pan and bake for 15 minutes. Reserve the remaining brownie mixture for the top.

While the bottom of the brownies bakes, mix the pumpkin cheesecake in a medium-sized mixing bowl. Beat the cream cheese until creamy. Add the pumpkin, egg, sugar, cinnamon, cloves, and ginger. Mix well.

When the 15 minutes is up, remove the pan form the oven and pour the pumpkin mixture over the top of the brownies. Drop the remaining half of the brownie batter by spoonful over the pumpkin batter. Use a knife to swirl the two together being careful not to stir up the cooked brownie bottom. Return the pan to the oven and bake for 24-27 minutes or until set. Allow brownies to cool on a wire rack for 1 hour. Then cover and refrigerate for 3-4 hours. Keep leftovers in an airtight container in the fridge.

Cakes and Pies

Birthdays aren't the only reason to bake a cake. A successful zucchini harvest is also a good reason. Don't believe me? Check out the recipe for Chocolate Zucchini cake on page 40. Graduations. Homecomings. Holidays. There is at least one reason per month to bake a moist, delicious cake for your family or a friend or a neighbor or a coworker. But really, do you need and excuse for cake? Try baking one on a Wednesday night and see how it goes over. I bet no one complains.

32 orange chocolate cake

35 chocolate dream pie

36 chocolate summer cake

39 chocolate almond cake

40 chocolate zucchini bundt cake

43 brownie bottom cheesecake

44 chocolate cheesecake

47 mom's best fudge cake

48 deep, dark, blue moon pie

51 chocolate cookie pie

58 chocolate heaven

orange chocolate cake

A dense cake such as this can be used for stacking. If you're going to stack the cake, instead of making it in a tube pan, then you'll need 3 (8-inch) round pans. Divide the batter and filling evenly and bake them for 17–20 minutes. Instead of layering the orange filling, you can swirl it into the batter still being careful that it doesn't touch the sides. I love recipes that can do more than one thing. They're like super-hero multitaskers.

serves 12

For the filling

¾ cup sweetened condensed milk (reserve the rest of the 14-oz. can for the glaze)	3 ounces cream cheese at room temperature	½ tsp. orange flavoring
	1 cup semi-sweet chocolate chips	1 tsp. vanilla flavoring

For the cake

4 ounces unsweetened baking chocolate	⅓ cup milk	1½ cups sugar
1 cup sour cream	1 tsp. vanilla	2 tsp. baking powder
½ cup butter at room temperature	3 eggs	½ tsp. baking soda
	2⅔ cups flour	½ tsp. salt

For the glaze

remaining sweetened condensed milk	1 Tbsp. butter	½ cup semi-sweet chocolate chips
	2 Tbsp. milk	

Directions

Grease and flour a 12-cup fluted tube cake pan the old fashioned way with shortening and flour. Set aside.

For the filling

In a small saucepan, melt ¾ cup of sweetened condensed milk, cream cheese, and chocolate chips. Once smooth, remove from heat and add the orange and vanilla flavoring. Set aside to cool while you make the cake batter.

For the cake

Preheat the oven to 350 degrees. Melt the baking chocolate over a double broiler. In a large mixing bowl, combine the chocolate, sour cream, butter, milk, vanilla and eggs. Add the flour, sugar, baking powder, soda, and salt. Beat until batter is smooth. Place three cups of batter in prepared pan and smooth to the edges. Pour half the chocolate filling over the batter being careful that it doesn't touch the sides. Cover the filling with batter and repeat the process. Smooth the top of the batter to the edges and seal in the filling. Bake for 50-65 minutes or until the center

springs back when lightly touched. Once done, allow to cool in the pan for 20 minutes. Invert the cake onto a serving platter and allow to cool completely.

For the glaze

Melt together the sweetened condensed milk, butter, milk and chocolate chips. Place the cake on a wire rack. Line a large cookie sheet with sides with wax paper and place a wire rack on top of the paper. Carefully place the cake on the wire rack. Now, drizzle the glaze over the cake and allow to set for 20-30 minutes before serving.

chocolate dream pie

Cream pies are always in season. You can make them for Thanksgiving or Valentine's Day or for a family picnic. In fact, this pie is so good, you're going to want to make it at least once a month. You can use this crust recipe or (gasp!) buy a premade crust at the store.

For Crust

1 ¼ cup flour	½ teaspoon salt	3-4 tablespoons cold water
½ cup butter, cold	½ teaspoon sugar	

For Pie Filling

1 ½ cups sugar	3 cups milk	2 tablespoons butter
1/3 cup cornstarch	4 egg yolks, beaten	
¼ teaspoon salt	1/3 cup cocoa	

For Topping

Whipped cream and chocolate shavings

Directions

For Crust

Place the flour, sugar, and salt in your food processor and pulse twice. Cut the butter into dime-size pieces and add half to the food processor. Pulse twice. Add the rest of the butter and pulse until the butter is the size of peas. Add 3 teaspoons of cold water and pulse again. Add more water and pulse stopping when the dough begins to hold together. Wrap the dough in plastic wrap and refrigerate for an hour.

Sprinkle your work surface with flour and place the ball of dough in the middle. Gently roll out the dough, starting in the middle and pressing out towards the edges until the dough is about 1/8 inch thick. Place the dough into the pie tin and gently form to the tin. Crimp and trim the edges of the pie and then stab with a fork in several places to allow steam to escape while the crust is cooking. Bake at 425 degrees for 10-13 minutes or until edges are slightly browned.

For Pie Filling

In a medium-sized saucepan, whisk together the sugar, cornstarch, salt, milk, and egg yolks until well combined. Cook over medium heat until mixture comes to a boil. Then stirring constantly, boil for 1 minute. Remove from the burner and add the cocoa and butter and stir well. Pour into the baked pie crust. Cover with plastic wrap, making sure the wrap touches the top of the pie, and refrigerate for 2 hours or until set. Top with whipped cream and chocolate shavings and serve.

chocolate summer cake

This cake must be served shortly after assembling for the best flavor and presentation. If you have leftovers, they should be kept, covered, in the refrigerator.

serves 8

Cake

½ cup butter at room temperature	⅓ cup milk	1 cup flour
½ cup sugar	1 tsp. vanilla	⅓ cup dark cocoa powder
4 egg yolks (reserve the whites for topping)	1 tsp. baking powder	½ tsp. salt

Topping

4 egg whites	1 cup sugar	½ cup chopped walnuts

Garnish

1½ cup whipping cream	1 tsp. vanilla	½ cup fudge sauce (recipe on page 125)
⅓ cup sugar	1 cup raspberries, strawberries, or blackberries	

For the cake

Preheat the oven to 325 degrees. Line two 8-inch round cake pans with aluminum foil and spray with nonstick cooking spray. Set aside.

Beat the butter and sugar together until fluffy, about three minutes. Add the egg yolks one at a time, beating between additions. Add the vanilla and milk and blend well. Add the baking powder, flour, cocoa, and salt and beat well. Divide batter between prepared pans spreading the batter to the edges. Set aside.

For the topping

In a medium-sized mixing bowl, beat the egg whites until stiff peaks form, about 5 minutes. Gently fold in the sugar and nuts. Divide the mixture in half and cover the cake batter in the prepared pans spreading mixture to the edges and leveling off the top. Cook for 60 minutes. Remove from the oven and allow to cool for 5-10 minutes. Using the foil, lift the cakes from the pans and allow to cool completely before assembling cake.

For the garnish

In a medium-sized mixing bowl, beat the whipping cream until thick, 5-8 minutes. Add the sugar and vanilla and beat until combined. Place one layer of cake on your serving platter. Spread half of the whipped cream over the cake. Drizzle half the chocolate on the whipped cream. Place the second layer on top of the whipped cream and repeat with the whipped cream and chocolate. Add fruit for garnish and serve. Keep the cake covered in the refrigerator.

chocolate almond cake

A favorite recipe! And it had better be because it can take up to 3 hours to assemble. However, those three hours are spread out throughout the day. So while the cake layers cool, you can run and errand or two. Also, the level of presentation makes a difference in the prep time. The more elaborate you are, the more time it will take.

serves 12

Cake

4 ounces unsweetened baking chocolate	4 Tbsp. butter	1 tsp. baking soda
3 Tbsp. cream	2 cups cake flour	1⅓ cups sugar
	1½ tsp. baking powder	3 eggs

Filling

¾ cup cream	½ cup milk chocolate chips	½ tsp. almond flavoring
¼ cup light corn syrup	½ cup dark chocolate chips	

Topping

chocolate buttercream frosting	chocolate-covered almonds for garnish
1½ cups chopped nuts	(at least 9 but more if you desire)

Directions

Preheat the oven to 325 degrees. Grease and flour two 8-inch round cake pans. Set aside.

Chop the baking chocolate into small pieces and place in the top of a double broiler. Add the cream and butter and melt together. Stir occasionally.

While the chocolate is melting, sift together the cake flour, baking powder, and baking soda in a large mixing bowl. Set aside.

In a medium-sized mixing bowl, beat together the sugar and eggs until they turn light yellow, about 1 minute. Add the melted chocolate mixture and mix just until combined. Pour the chocolate/egg mixture into the flour bowl and mix well. The batter will be thick. Pour batter into prepared pans. Cook for 20 minutes or until a toothpick inserted in the center comes out clean. Run a knife around the inside edge of the cake pan. Allow the cakes to cool for 10 minutes before inverting the layers onto a wire rack to cool before stacking.

To prepare the filling by mixing the cream and corn syrup in a saucepan over medium heat. Once the mixture starts to boil, remove it from the heat. Pour the chocolate chips into a heat-proof bowl and pour the cream mixture over them. Allow to sit for five minutes then stir until smooth. Add the almond flavoring. Set the mixture in the fridge for 45–60 minutes, stirring every 15 minutes. Take the chocolate out of the fridge and whip until thick. Quickly spread over the bottom layer of cake. Place the top layer on the filling and place the cake in the refrigerator for 1 hour to set. Frost with chocolate buttercream frosting and garnish with chopped nuts and chocolate covered almonds.

chocolate zucchini
bundt cake

There's an old joke about not leaving your car unlocked at church during the zucchini harvest because well-meaning neighbors will share their bounty and you'll be stuck with a carload of zucchini. With this recipe in your arsenal, you'll be praying for zucchini to rain down from heaven. You can top it with the cherry pie filling but it's also wonderful with the chocolate glaze (page 120) or drizzled with fudge sauce (page 125). If you like, you can add 1 cup of nuts and/or 1 cup chocolate chips to the batter before baking. It's really a versatile recipe and the most delicious way to eat your vegetables.

serves 16

Ingredients

5 medium zucchini	2 tsp. vanilla	1½ tsp. baking powder
2¼ cups sugar	2⅔ cups flour	2¼ tsp. baking soda
4 eggs	¾ cup cocoa	1 (21-oz.) can cherry pie filling, optional
1½ cups canola oil	2¼ tsp. cinnamon	

Directions

Preheat the oven to 325 degrees. Spray a bunt cake pan or tube cake pan with nonstick cooking spray. Dust with flour. Or, mix 1 teaspoon of cocoa powder in with ¼ flour and use that mixture to dust your pan.

Peal the zucchini and shred it. Use a small cheese grater or a food processor to get small pieces. Place the shredded zucchini in a bowl and allow to sit while you mix up the batter.

In a large mixing bowl, beat together the sugar, eggs, and oil for 5 minutes. Squeeze the zucchini to remove excess water and place the zucchini in the batter. Discard the liquid. Add the vanilla and mix well.

In a separate bowl, sift together the flour, cocoa, cinnamon, baking powder, and baking soda. Slowly add to the zucchini mixture and mix just until combined. Pour into the prepared pan and bake for 75-80 minutes or until a toothpick inserted near the center comes out clean. Cool in the pan for 30 minutes before inverting. Allow to cool completely before slicing and serving with cherry topping.

brownie bottom cheesecake

You can top this cake with the white chocolate drizzle on page 125 and fruit for an elegant presentation. Or, you can use a fruit sauce, like strawberry, nuts and hot fudge. Whipped cream with a dusting of cocoa powder is also delicious.

serves 12

Brownie

½ cup butter, melted

⅓ cup cocoa powder

1 cup sugar

2 eggs

1 tsp. vanilla

¾ cup flour

Cheesecake

¾ cup semi-sweet chocolate chips

2 (8-oz.) packages cream cheese

2 Tbsp. sour cream

½ cup sugar

2 Tbsp. cocoa powder

2 eggs

15-20 ice cubes

white chocolate drizzle (page 125), optional

fruit (optional)

For the brownie layer

Preheat the oven to 350 degrees. Spray a large springform pan with nonstick cooking spray and set aside.

Combine the melted butter, cocoa, and sugar. Add the eggs and vanilla and stir well. Add the flour and mix until just combined scraping down the sides as you stir. Pour the batter into the prepared pan and smooth out. Bake for 20-25 minutes or until a toothpick inserted in the center comes out clean. Remove from oven and allow to cool while making the cheesecake.

For cheesecake layer

In a small saucepan, melt the chocolate chips over low heat. Once the chocolate is smooth with no lumps, remove from the heat and set aside.

In a medium-sized mixing bowl, beat the cream cheese until smooth. Add the sour cream, sugar and cocoa powder and beat well. Add the eggs one at a time beating well between additions. Pour the batter over the brownies and smooth. Place the pan back in the oven. Add the ice cubes to the bottom of the oven. They will steam and help keep the cheesecake from cracking on the top as it cooks. Bake for 30-35 minutes or until a knife inserted in the center comes out clean. Once the cake is done, remove the pan from the oven and allow the cake to cool for 30-45 minutes at room temperature or until the bottom of the pan is only slightly warm. Cover the cake and place it in the refrigerator for 4 hours or overnight. Drizzle with white chocolate topping (recipe on page 125) and add fruit if desired.

chocolate cheesecake

It is imperative that the cream cheese in this recipe be at room temperature before beating. If it isn't, the cheesecake will have lumps. I know it's cheesecake, and no one would turn it down, but lumpy cheesecake will not have the same power as a creamy, dreamy dessert. If you're in a hurry, you can place the cream cheese in a microwave-safe dish and "warm" it in the microwave at half power for 30 second intervals. Do not overcook! It's a fine line.

serves 12

Ingredients

2 cups crushed chocolate wafer cookies (about 12 cookies)

3 Tbsp. butter, melted

2 Tbsp. sugar

2 ounces unsweetened baking chocolate

3 (8-oz.) packages cream cheese, at room temperature

¾ cups sugar

2 eggs

1½ tsp. vanilla

1 cup ice cubes

Directions

Spray a 9-inch springform pan with nonstick cooking spray. Set aside. To make the crust, stir together the crushed cookies, butter, and sugar. Press mixture into the bottom of the prepared pan. Set aside.

Preheat the oven to 350 degrees.

Chop the baking chocolate into small chunks. Place the chocolate in the top of a double broiler and melt, stirring occasionally. Set aside to cool slightly.

Beat the cream cheese and sugar together until smooth. Add the eggs one at a time beating well between each addition. Finally, add the vanilla and mix well. Pour batter into prepared pan. Smooth out the top. Spread 1 cup of ice cubes in the bottom of your oven. As they melt and evaporate, they will provide moisture for the cheesecake and help keep it from cracking. Place the cake in the oven and cook for 60–70 minutes or until the center is set. Remove from oven and allow to cool for 5 minutes. Run a knife around the inside of the pan. Place the pan in the fridge for 2 hours. Cover and allow to refrigerate for another 2 hours or overnight. Serve with chocolate sauce.

mom's best
fudge cake

As the name indicates, this recipe came from my mother, an excellent cook and baker. This light and moist cake is excellent for birthdays. However, it is not good for stacking, trust me, I've tried.

serves 24

Ingredients

3 Tbsp. butter
⅓ cup cocoa
1⅔ cup sugar, divided
1½ cup milk, divided

3 eggs, divided
½ cup shortening
1 tsp. vanilla
2 cups flour

1 tsp. baking soda
½ tsp. salt
Fudge Frosting
(recipe on page 124)

Directions

Preheat the oven to 350 degrees. Line a 10½ × 15½-inch jelly roll pan with aluminum foil and spray with nonstick cooking spray. Set aside.

In a medium-sized saucepan, melt the butter over low heat. Remove the pan from the burner and add the cocoa powder, ⅔ cup sugar, ½ cup milk, and 1 egg. Stir well. Return the pan to the stovetop and increase the heat to medium. Cook and stir just until the mixture comes to a boil. Remove from the heat and set aside.

In a large mixing bowl, cream the shortening and remaining cup of sugar until light and fluffy. Add the vanilla and the last two eggs, one at a time, beating well after each addition. Now you can add in the flour, baking soda, salt, and 1 cup milk. Mix well. While the mixer is going, pour in the chocolate mixture. Transfer the batter to the prepared pan, smooth the batter to the edges, and bake for 20-25 minutes or until a toothpick inserted in the center comes out clean. Frost with Fudge Frosting if desired.

deep, dark, blue moon pie

For the dark chocolate lovers out there.

serves 8

Ingredients

1 pie crust, cooked

1 (8-oz.) package cream cheese at room temperature

¼ cup sugar

1 cup milk chocolate chips

1 cup extra dark chocolate chips

1 Tbsp. butter

1½ cups whipping cream

4 Tbsp. powdered sugar

1 tsp. vanilla

chocolate curls or shavings

Directions

In a large mixing bowl, beat the cream cheese until smooth. Add the sugar and beat well. Set aside.

Place the chocolate chips and butter in a saucepan and melt over low heat, stirring occasionally.

While the chocolate melts, whip the cream in a separate bowl until soft peaks form. Add the powdered sugar and vanilla and beat well.

Once the chocolate melts, combine the cream cheese mixture, the chocolate, and 1½ cups of the whipped cream. Transfer to the prepared pie crust and spread. Refrigerate at least one hour. Top with the remaining whipped cream and chocolate curls or shavings.

chocolate cookie pie

Cream-filled cookies are always a treat. When mixed into this pie, they become the magic ingredient.

serves 8

Ingredients

1 (9-inch) pie crust	3 eggs	1 tsp. vanilla
¾ cup butter at room temperature	1 cup brown sugar	12 sandwich cookies, divided
2 ounces cream cheese at room temperature	2½ ounces unsweetened baking chocolate	2 cups whipped cream

Directions

Prepare the pie crust according to package directions and set aside to cool.

In a medium-sized mixing bowl, beat together the butter and cream cheese, set aside.

In a small saucepan, whip together the eggs and brown sugar. Heat over low until the sugar melts, 5-7 minutes, increase the temperature to medium, stirring constantly. Just as the mixture comes to a boil, or reaches 160 degrees, remove from heat. Break the baking chocolate into dime-sized pieces. Add the chocolate to the hot egg mixture and allow to sit for 5 minutes. Stir until the chocolate melts. Add the chocolate mixture and vanilla to the butter mixture and beat until smooth. Chop 6 cookies into bite-sized pieces and add to the pie filling. Stir until just combined and then pour into the prepared pie crust. Cover with plastic wrap and refrigerate for 3 hours. Top with whipped cream and remaining cookies before serving.

chocolate heaven

This multi-tiered dessert is sure to please every chocolate lover you know. It's so good, it could convert people to chocolate. It's also easy to make. Although there are several steps and it does take some time, none of the steps are complicated. That may mean it's a special occasion dessert, but oh what an occasion it will be with Chocolate Heaven on the menu.

serves 12

Ingredients

1 batch of One-Bag Chocolate Ganache (recipe on page 121)	3 cups fresh whipped cream	strawberry slices for garnish

Cake

6 eggs	1 Tbsp. vanilla	2 tsp. baking soda
2 cups sugar	1½ cup flour	¼ tsp. salt
⅔ cups water	¾ cup cocoa powder	

Chocolate Filling

1½ cups semi-sweet chocolate chips	1 Tbsp. butter	¼ cup cocoa powder
	1½ cups + 2 Tbsp. cream, divided	

Directions

Line two 15 × 10-inch jelly roll pans with aluminum foil and spray with nonstick cooking spray. Set aside. Preheat the oven to 375 degrees.

In a large mixing bowl, beat the eggs for 3 minutes on high speed. While the mixer is running, slowly add the sugar, then water and vanilla. Stop the mixer and add the flour, cocoa, baking soda, and salt. Mix until just combined scraping down the sides of the bowl as necessary. Divide the batter between the two prepared pans and bake for 17–22 minutes or until a toothpick inserted in the center comes out clean.

Allow the cakes to cool completely.

To make the filling, melt the chocolate chips, butter, and 2 tablespoons of the cream together, stirring occasionally. Once the mixture is smooth, place it in the fridge for 30 minutes.

Once the chocolate mixture has cooled, add ½ cup of cream and beat until smooth. Add the cocoa powder and remaining cup of cream and beat until stiff peaks form.

To assemble the dessert, invert one of the cakes onto a large serving platter and cut off the edges. Spread half of the chocolate mousse on the cake and then half of the whipped cream. Drizzle half of the chocolate ganache over the top. Repeat layers and garnish with strawberries to finish.

Cookies

57 chocolate chunk cookies

58 world's most addictive cookie

61 mint chocolate cookies

68 rolayne's chocolate chip cookies

65 coconut and chocolate cookies

66 blueberry and white chocolate cookies

69 dark chocolate cookies

70 oatmeal pan cookies

73 chocolate and peanut butter cookies

74 chocolate fudge cookies

77 chocolate almond press cookies

chocolate chunk cookies

Use milk chocolate in these cookies for a traditional chocolate cookie flavor or semi-sweet for a brush with the dark side.

makes 36 cookies

Ingredients

1 cup butter at room temperature	¾ brown sugar	1 tsp. soda
¾ cup sugar	1 egg	1 tsp. salt
	2¼ cups flour	2 cups chopped chocolate

Directions

Preheat oven to 375 degrees.

In a medium-sized mixing bowl, beat the butter, sugar, brown sugar and egg. Add the flour, soda, and salt and mix well. Stir the chocolate pieces in by hand. Place 1-inch balls of dough 2 inches apart on a cookie sheet. Bake for 9-11 minutes or until set. Remove from cookie sheet and allow to cool on a wire rack.

world's most addictive cookie

With a cookie that is de-vine, a perfectly sweet layer of caramel, and a garnish of smooth milk chocolate, these cookies are too good to let go. If you're making them as a gift, you may want to double the recipe as, once done, they can be darn-near impossible to part with.

makes 24 cookies

Ingredients

1 cup butter, at room temperature	½ tsp. salt	1 Tbsp. whipping cream
½ cup powdered sugar	1 tsp. vanilla	1 cup milk chocolate chips
¼ cup cocoa powder	2 cups flour	1 Tbsp. butter
	1 (11-oz.) package caramels	

Directions

Beat the butter, powdered sugar, and cocoa powder together in a large mixing bowl. Add the salt, vanilla, and flour and mix until the dough comes together. Form the dough into a long worm, wrap in plastic wrap and chill for 1–2 hours.

Preheat the oven to 350 degrees. Slice the dough into ¼-inch sections and place 1 inch apart on a cookie sheet. Bake for 10–12 minutes or until set.

In a medium-sized saucepan, melt the caramels and whipping cream together over medium-low heat. Stir occasionally until the caramels start to melt. Then, stir more often to keep them from scorching. Drop one spoonful of caramel onto each cookie.

In a small saucepan, melt the chocolate chips and butter together until smooth. Drop one spoonful of chocolate over each cookie. Use the back of the spoon to spread the chocolate around and smooth the top. Allow to set at room temperature.

mint chocolate cookies

One of the things I love about these cookies is that they are versatile. For example, you can make them with the melted mint tops or leave off the mint and they make a wonderful ice cream sandwich cookie, a frosting sandwich cookie, or just eat them plain. I chose to present the mint version here, because they are simply wonderful.

makes 36 cookies

Ingredients

¾ cup butter	2 eggs	1¼ tsp. baking soda
1½ cup brown sugar	1 tsp. vanilla	1 tsp. salt
2 cups semi-sweet chocolate chips	2½ cups flour	36 mint chocolate candies, unwrapped

Directions

In a medium-sized saucepan, melt together the butter and brown sugar. Once the butter is melted, remove the pan from the stove and add the chocolate chips. Stir 4 times and set aside for 10 minutes to cool. The chocolate may not melt all the way but that's okay.

Meanwhile, in a large mixing bowl, combine the flour, baking soda, and salt. Set aside. Add the eggs and vanilla to the chocolate mixture then add the chocolate mixture to the flour mixture. Cover and chill the dough for 30 minutes in the freezer.

Preheat the oven to 350 degrees. Use a cookie scoop or tablespoon to make even-sized balls of dough. Place them 2 inches apart on an ungreased cookie sheet and bake for 9–11 minutes or until set. Remove the cookie sheet from the oven and place a mint wafer on top. Return sheet to the oven for 30 seconds–1 minute.

Use the back side of a metal spoon to spread the mint chocolate across of the cookie. Making small circles seems to work best. Remove the cookies from the cookie sheet and allow to cool on a wire rack.

rolayne's chocolate chip cookies

The chocolate chip cookie is a basic for every chocolate lover's cookie jar. What I love about this recipe, is that the dough can be frozen in ball shape and then cooked right out of the freezer. What, you need a dozen cookies for the bake sale? Bam! Had a bad day at school? Have a cookie right from the oven. Chocolate craving? Warm cookies are only 13 minutes away.

Once you mix up the dough, you can bake a batch right away as a reward and then freeze the rest for emergency cookie situations later. Frozen dough can stay in the freezer for up to 30 days.

makes 80 cookies

Ingredients

3 eggs	2 tsp. vanilla	1½ cups oatmeal
2 cups sugar	6 cups flour	4 cups chocolate chips, any kind
2 cups brown sugar	1½ teaspoon baking soda	
1 pound butter, melted	1½ teaspoon salt	

Directions

In a large mixing bowl, beat the eggs until frothy. Add the sugar, brown sugar, butter and vanilla and mix well. Then add the flour, baking soda and salt. Finally, mix in the oatmeal and chocolate chips.

Line a cookie sheet with wax paper. Roll the dough into 1-inch balls placing them on the cookie sheet. You can set them right next to one another. Freeze for 2 hours or overnight and then divide them into large zip-top freezer bags for storage.

To bake, preheat the oven to 350 degrees. Place the frozen cookie balls on a cookie sheet and bake for 13 minutes or until lightly browned. Do not overbake.

coconut and chocolate cookies

Chewy and filling, it doesn't take many of these delicious cookies to satiate your chocolate craving.

makes 36 cookies

Ingredients

¾ cup butter

¾ cup brown sugar

⅓ cup sugar

1 tsp. vanilla

1 egg

2 ounces baking chocolate, melted

1 tsp. baking powder

½ tsp. baking soda

½ tsp. salt

1⅔ cup flour

1 cup white chocolate chips

1 cup semi-sweet chocolate chips

1 cup shredded coconut

¾ cup chopped walnuts

Directions

Preheat the oven to 350 degrees.

In a medium-sized mixing bowl, beat the butter, brown sugar, and sugar together. Add the vanilla and egg and beat for 2 minutes. Now add the melted chocolate, baking powder, baking soda, salt and flour. Mix until well combined. Stir in the chocolate chips, coconut, and walnuts. Roll into 1-inch balls or use a cookie scoop to divide the batter into even amounts on an ungreased cookie sheet. Bake for 8-10 minutes or until set.

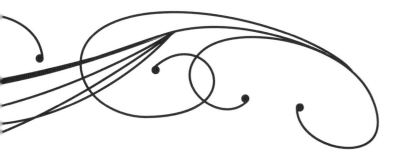

blueberry and white chocolate cookies

If these cookies have a fault, it's that there is too many mix-ins. You'll need to be careful to put enough cookie batter with the chocolate chips and blueberries to hold the cookies together as they bake. Of course, if they crumble, you can always use them as an ice cream topper.

makes 36 cookies

Ingredients

2 cups butter

1 cup brown sugar

2 eggs

1 tsp. vanilla

½ cup cocoa powder

1 tsp. baking soda

1 tsp. salt

1¾ cups oats

2 cups flour

1 cup whole wheat flour

1½ cups dried blueberries

1 cup white chocolate chips

1 cup semi-sweet chocolate chips

Directions

Preheat the oven to 375 degrees.

In a medium-sized mixing bowl, beat together the butter, brown sugar, eggs and vanilla. Mix in the cocoa powder, baking soda, and salt. Add the oats, flour, and wheat flour and mix until well combined. Stir in the blueberries, white chocolate chips and semi-sweet chocolate by hand. Roll into 1-inch balls or use a cookie scoop to divide out the batter and place on a cookie sheet leaving space between cookies. Bake for 8-10 minutes or until set.

dark chocolate cookies

These cookies have just enough of a sweet flavor to keep them from tasting bitter, but the cocoa comes through loud and clear. If you're the type who enjoys dark chocolates, then these are the cookies for you. You can change out the milk chocolate chips for all semi-sweet or even white if you prefer.

makes 36 cookies

Ingredients

⅓ cup butter

¾ cup brown sugar

¼ cup sugar

2 eggs

1 tsp. vanilla

1½ cups flour

¼ cup special dark cocoa powder

1 tsp. baking powder

¼ tsp. salt

1 cup semi-sweet chocolate chips

½ cup milk chocolate chips

Directions

In a medium-sized mixing bowl, cream the butter, brown sugar, and sugar together. Add the eggs and vanilla and mix well. Beat in the flour, cocoa, baking powder and salt until the batter is smooth. Add the chocolate chips and stir in by hand. Cover the bowl with plastic wrap and refrigerate for 30-45 minutes. Preheat the oven to 350 degrees. Use a large cookie scoop to form 2-inch balls of dough and place them on a cookie sheet. Bake for 10-12 minutes or until centers are set. Allow to cool for 1 minute on the cookie sheet before transferring to a wire rack to complete the cooling process.

oatmeal pan cookies

This is another recipe from my mom. She was tired of making cookies in 8-minute intervals and wanted a one-pan oatmeal cookie. Besides mixing in one bowl and cooking in one pan, the cookies freeze and travel well.

makes 32 bar cookies

Ingredients

1 cup of butter at room temperature

¾ cup sugar

¾ cup brown sugar

1 tsp. vanilla

2 eggs

1 cup flour

1 tsp. baking soda

1 tsp. salt

3 cups uncooked oats (Mom uses regular, but quick oats will work too)

2 cups milk chocolate chips

½ cup butterscotch chips (optional)

1 cup chopped walnuts (optional)

Directions

Preheat the oven to 375 degrees. Spray a 9 × 13 inch pan with nonstick cooking spray and set aside.

In a large mixing bowl, beat the butter, sugar, and brown sugar until creamy. Add the vanilla and eggs and mix well. Gradually add the flour, baking soda, and salt. Incorporate the oats. Stir the chocolate chips, butterscotch chips, and nuts in by hand. Transfer the dough to the prepared pan. Use the back of a metal spoon to spread the dough to the corners of the pan. Bake for 20-25 minutes or until the top of the cookie is golden but not brown, the middle may not look set. If using a glass pan, reduce the oven temperature to 350 degrees.

chocolate and peanut butter cookies

Made like traditional peanut butter cookies, this chocolate version takes the flavor one step higher.

makes 36 cookies

Ingredients

2 oz. baking chocolate

½ cup butter at room temperature

½ cup creamy peanut butter

½ cup sugar

½ cup brown sugar

2 eggs

1¼ cups flour

½ tsp. baking soda

½ tsp. salt

½ cup peanut butter chips for garnish

Directions

Preheat the oven to 350 degrees.

Melt the baking chocolate in a double broiler. Set aside.

In a large mixing bowl, cream together the butter, peanut butter, sugar and brown sugar. Add the eggs and mix well. Add the flour, baking soda and salt and mix until well combined. Use a cookie scoop to portion out dough onto an ungreased cookie sheet. Bake for 10–12 minutes or until centers are set. Remove from the cookie sheet and allow to cool. Melt the peanut butter chips in the microwave at half power for 1–4 minutes stopping each minute to stir. Transfer the melted chips to a plastic sandwich bag and snip off the corner. Make 3 stripes in one direction and 3 stripes crossing them. Allow the melted peanut butter chips to set before storing.

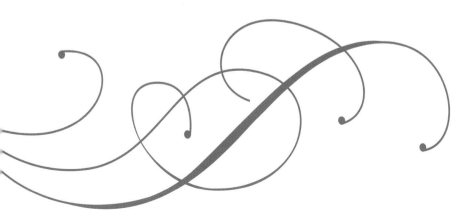

chocolate
fudge cookies

Adorable cookies worthy of any tea party, luncheon, or brunch.

makes 24 cookies

Ingredients

1 ounce unsweetened chocolate

½ cup butter flavored shortening

½ cup sugar

1 egg, separated

1 tsp. vanilla

½ tsp. salt

1 cup flour

¾ cup chopped walnuts or chocolate sprinkles

2 ounces white chocolate (optional)

Directions

Preheat the oven to 350 degrees.

Melt the chocolate in a double broiler, set aside.

In a medium-sized mixing bowl, beat the shortening until fluffy. Add the chocolate and mix. Add the sugar, egg yolk, vanilla, salt, and flour to the chocolate mixture. Beat with a hand mixer until the dough turns a dark chocolate brown and clumps together.

In a small bowl, beat the egg white and set aside.

Place the nuts or sprinkles on a plate.

Use a small cookie scoop to make teaspoon-sized balls from the dough. Roll the balls in the egg white and then in the nuts or sprinkles. Place on an ungreased cookie sheet. Repeat with remaining dough. Bake for 10-12 minutes or until cookies are set. Transfer cookies to a wire rack to cool. Once cooled, drizzle with white chocolate, if desired.

chocolate almond
press cookies

Crispy, like an English biscuit, these cookies are great for dunking in a cup of hot chocolate.

makes 60 cookies

Ingredients

2½ ounces unsweetened chocolate, melted

½ cup butter at room temperature

1 cup sugar

1 egg

3-4 Tbsp. cream, divided

2 cups flour

½ tsp. salt

Directions

Preheat the oven to 400 degrees.

Melt the chocolate over a double broiler. Set aside.

In a medium-sized mixing bowl, beat the butter, sugar, and egg for three minutes. Add three tablespoons of cream, flour, and salt. Mix until combined. If needed, add the last tablespoon of cream to make the dough loose enough to go through a cookie press. Prepare the cookie press and fill with dough. Press dough onto a cookie sheet leaving ½ inch between cookies. Bake for 8-10 minutes or until edges are set. Remove from cookie sheet and allow to cool.

Desserts

Wait, aren't all the recipes in this book considered desserts? They are all sweet or decadent and full of chocolate—so yeah, they could all work for a final course.

However, brownies and cookies are more likely to be consumed at 10:00 a.m. or 3:00 p.m. as a snack around our house. And sometimes, if the recipe has oatmeal, I might just eat it for breakfast. But the recipes in this section are desserts that can be presented. You can serve them after a meal or at a baby or bridal shower, a block party, or any number of occasions.

81   simple chocolate ice cream

82   s'mores ice cream

85   peanut butter & chocolate tart

86   toffee bottom fudge tart

89   chocolate tart

90   chocolate pudding

93   chocolate twists

94   chocolate crêpes

97   cream pops

98   mini chocolate chip muffins

simple chocolate
ice cream

Every so often, it's good to get back to basics. This ice cream, though simple with few ingredients, has a classic chocolate taste and flavor. You can serve it on a cone, or use it for a banana split. No matter how you serve it, you'll be glad you have the recipe on hand.

serves 6

Ingredients

2 ounces unsweetened chocolate	1 cup heavy cream ¾ cup sugar	2½ cups whole milk 1 tsp. vanilla

Directions

Chop the chocolate into small slivers. Heat the chocolate and the heavy cream in a large saucepan over medium heat until the chocolate melts. Use a whisk to incorporate the chocolate. The mixture shouldn't come anywhere near a boil and if there are tiny chocolate flakes left, it's okay.

Continue to heat on the stove and add the sugar and milk and whisk until smooth. Once small bubbles start to form around the inside edge of the pan, remove the pan from the heat and stir in the vanilla. Cover the pan and place it in the refrigerator for 2-4 hours.

Once chilled, pour the mixture into your ice cream maker and follow the manufacturer's instructions. It usually takes 20-25 minutes for the ice cream to freeze to a soft-serve consistence.

You can serve it immediately in bowls, or you can place it in a plastic container with a lid and freeze to harden it enough to serve on a cone.

s'mores ice cream

I must admit, I have a huge soft spot for s'mores. Perhaps it's because s'mores aren't just a flavor, they are an experience. When you make a s'more over an open fire, you're usually with friends, you've spent the day in the great outdoors pleasantly exhausting your body, and the crickets chirp a soft hello. I hope, when you taste this ice cream, you'll gain a whisper of the s'mores experience.

serves 8

Ingredients

4 egg yolks
⅓ cup heavy cream
¾ cup sugar

2¼ cups whole milk
½ cup cocoa powder
6 graham crackers, crushed

1 Tbsp. butter, melted
12 regular-sized marshmallows

Directions

Place the egg yolks and cream in a blender. Pulse until smooth. Don't over do it, just make sure the egg yolks are beaten well. The mixture should be a pale yellow color. Add the sugar and the milk and pulse again. Pour the liquid into a medium-sized saucepan and bring to a simmer over medium heat. Remove the pan from the stove and whisk in the cocoa powder. Once the cocoa is incorporated, return the pan to the stove and heat until the mixture thickens. Whisk constantly while cooking. It should only take 3-5 minutes to thicken. Pour the mixture into a new bowl and refrigerate for 2 hours.

In the meantime, place the crushed graham crackers in a small bowl and add the butter. Stir together to coat the crumbs with the butter. Set aside.

Once the ice cream has cooled, pour it into your ice cream maker and follow the manufacturer's instructions for making the ice cream.

While the ice cream is setting, place the marshmallows in a medium-sized pan and melt half-way. You'll want some bumps to remain. Remove from heat and set aside. When the ice cream is at soft-serve consistency, pour ¼ of the ice cream into a plastic container. Layer ¼ of the graham cracker mixture and ¼ of the marshmallows over the top. Use a large knife to swirl them together. Then repeat 3 more times with the remaining ¾ of ingredients. Place the ice cream in the freezer for 4-6 hours to set before serving.

peanut butter & chocolate tart

There is a great love out there in the world for all things peanut butter and chocolate. If you're one of the millions who savor the sweet and salty combination, then you'll love this tart which has a one in a million flavor.

serves 12

Crust

½ cup butter	1 cup flour	1 tsp. vanilla
⅓ cup powdered sugar		

Peanut Butter Layer

2 Tbsp. butter	½ cup powdered sugar	½ tsp. salt
1 cup super-chunky peanut butter	1 tsp. vanilla	10 regular-sized marshmallows

Chocolate Layer

1 cup milk chocolate chips	2 Tbsp. butter-flavored shortening	a pinch of salt

For the crust

Spray a round tart pan with nonstick cooking spray and set aside.

In a medium-sized mixing bowl, beat together the butter, powdered sugar, flour, and vanilla until the mixture forms marble-sized balls. Press the dough into the prepared pan and pierce with a fork. Refrigerate for 30 minutes. Preheat the oven to 350 degrees and bake the crust for 10-15 minutes or until set but not browned.

For the peanut butter layer

In a medium-sized saucepan, melt the butter, peanut butter, and marshmallows together. Add the powdered sugar and vanilla and stir well. Pour the peanut butter mixture into the cooked crust and spread out evenly.

For the chocolate layer

In a small saucepan, melt the chocolate and shortening together. Once cooked, add the salt and stir well. Pour the chocolate over the top of the peanut butter layer. Spread with an off-set spatula then shimmy the pan so that there are no marks in the chocolate. Allow the tart to set at room temperature for 4 hours or place in the refrigerator for 60-90 minutes or until the layers are set. To cut, heat a knife by running it under hot water for a few seconds. Wipe the water away, then cut the pastry.

toffee bottom
fudge tart

While I recommend walnuts in the recipe, because they are my personal favorite, I've also made this with pecans and gotten a good response. The filling gives just enough of a caramel flavor to tease your taste buds.

serves 12

Crust

5 Tbsp. butter at room temperature	⅔ cup brown sugar	1⅓ cups flour

Nut Filling

½ cup butter	¾ cup brown sugar	1 cup walnut halves

Chocolate Filling

12 ounces semi-sweet chocolate	2 Tbsp. cream	1 cup sweetened condensed milk

For the Crust

In a medium-sized mixing bowl, beat together the butter, sugar, and flour until it resembles a course meal. Press the mixture into the bottom and sides of a round tart pan.

For the Nut Filling

Preheat the oven to 350 degrees. Arrange the walnut halves in the bottom of the crust. In a small saucepan, melt the butter and brown sugar over medium heat. Bring to a boil and boil for 30 seconds stirring continuously. Once done, pour over the nuts in the bottom of the pan. Bake for 20 minutes. Remove from oven and allow to cool while you make the chocolate filling.

For the Chocolate Filling

In a medium-sized saucepan, melt the chocolate, cream, and sweetened condensed milk. Stir occasionally and remove from heat once smooth. Allow to set at room temperature for 2–4 hours before cutting.

chocolate tart

This tart is an easy dessert that looks like it took a long time. Your family will think you slaved all day when in reality, the pan does most of the work for presentation. If you'd like, you can sprinkle the top of the tart with ¼ cup chopped almonds as a garnish.

serves 8

Crust

½ cup butter at room temperature	3 Tbsp. sugar	¼ tsp. salt
	1 tsp. vanilla	1¼ cups flour

Filling

1½ cup cream	¾ pounds semi-sweet chocolate, chopped	½ tsp. almond flavoring

Directions

In a medium-sized mixing bowl, beat together the butter, sugar, vanilla and salt. Add all the flour at once and beat until it becomes a course meal. Press the dough into the bottom and up the sides of a rectangle tart pan with removable bottom. Cover the pan with plastic wrap and refrigerate for 30 minutes. Remove from the fridge and poke the bottom and sides of the dough generously with a fork. Bake for 20-25 minutes at 350 degrees or until center is set but the edges aren't brown. Allow to cool before filling.

While the crust cooks, you can make the filling. Pour the cream into a small saucepan and cook over medium-low heat until it starts to steam but not boil. Remove from heat, add the chocolate, and allow to sit for 5 minutes. Stir until smooth and then add the almond flavoring. Allow to cool to room temperature before pouring into the prepared crust. Allow to set in the refrigerator for 2-4 hours before serving.

chocolate pudding

There is a big difference between chocolate pudding out of the box and chocolate pudding made from scratch. Pudding made from scratch has a much more chocolate flavor and tastes less sweet. This recipe can be made and served with a topping of fruit and whipped cream or in a dessert such as a trifle.

serves 6

Ingredients

2 ounces unsweetened baking chocolate

¾ cup brown sugar

¼ cup sugar

¼ cup cornstarch

2½ cups milk

3 egg yolks, beaten

1 Tbsp. butter

1 tsp. vanilla

fresh fruit, chocolate curls, and/or whipped cream for serving

Directions

In the top pan of a double boiler over medium heat, melt the baking chocolate. Add the brown sugar, sugar, cornstarch, and milk. Cook, whisking to incorporate the chocolate, until the sugars dissolve.

Add ½ cup of the chocolate mixture to the egg yolks and beat well. Whisk while you pour the egg mixture into the chocolate mixture on the stove. Move the pan off the double broiler and set it on the stove top over medium heat. Stir continuously as the mixture comes to a boil. Boil 1 minute and then remove immediately from the heat.

Add the butter and vanilla and stir until the butter is melted. Allow the pudding to cool for 5 minutes. Cover with plastic wrap making sure the plastic touches the top of the pudding. Cool in the refrigerator for 2 hours or overnight before serving. Top with fresh fruit, whipped cream, or chocolate curls to serve.

chocolate twists

These light and flaky twists are a sweet and chocolatey. Though they look elegant, they don't take much time to prepare. Once you get the hang of twisting the dough, the process goes smoothly.

makes 14

Ingredients

2 cups flour
2 Tbsp. sugar
1 Tbsp. baking powder
½ tsp. salt

½ cup butter at room temperature plus 2 Tbsp., divided
1 egg
½ cup milk plus 1 Tbsp.,

divided
¼ cup brown sugar
½ cup chocolate chips
½ cup powdered sugar

Directions

Preheat the oven to 450 degrees. Line a cookie sheet with a nonstick baking mat.

In a medium-sized mixing bowl, stir together the flour, sugar, baking powder, and salt. Add the butter and use a hand mixer or standing mixer to combine.

Once the mixture resembles coarse crumbs, add the egg and ½ cup of milk and mix together. Place dough on a lightly floured surface and roll out to a 14 × 8-inch rectangle. Melt 1 tablespoon of butter in a small bowl in the microwave and spread over half the dough.

Fold the dough in half lengthwise so cover one long side with the butter. Sprinkle the buttered side with the brown sugar and chocolate chips. Fold the ungarnished side of the dough over the toppings and press the edges to seal. Cut the dough into 14 strips. Twist each strip 3 times and lay on prepared cookie sheet.

Bake for 8-10 minutes or until lightly browned. Remove from oven. Melt the remaining tablespoon of butter and add the powdered sugar and remaining tablespoon of milk. Stir together to make a glaze and brush over the warm twists. Serve warm or cold.

chocolate crêpes

While this recipe is meant for a dessert dish, you can certainly serve it for breakfast. Just leave out the marshmallow filling and substitute with chunky or smooth peanut butter or just the whipped cream and fruit will do.

serves 6

Ingredients

1 ½ cups milk

2 Tbsp. canola oil

3 eggs

1 tsp. vanilla

¼ cup sugar

1 ½ cup flour

2 Tbsp. dark cocoa

pinch of salt

1 batch of Marshmallow Filling (recipe on page 120)

strawberries, blueberries, bananas or other fruit cut into bite-sized pieces (3 cups)

whipped cream

chocolate sprinkles

Directions

In a medium-sized mixing bowl, combine the milk, oil, eggs, vanilla, sugar, flour, dark cocoa, and salt. Once the mixture is smooth, turn of the beaters and let it sit for 20 minutes.

Place a crêpes pan on the stove and warm over medium heat.

Once the mixture has set, pour 3-4 tablespoons into warmed crêpes pan and swirl the pan to coat the bottom. Cook the batter until the top appears dry. Flip the crêpe and cook the other side for 10-15 seconds. Remove the crêpe from the pan and fill with Marshmallow Filling, fruit slices, whipped cream, and chocolate sprinkles. Serve warm.

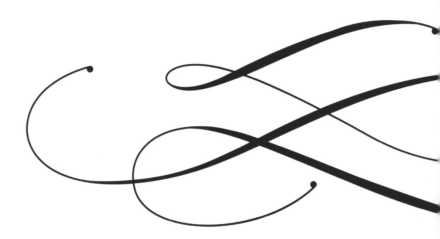

cream pops

Nothing beats a creamy frozen chocolate treat on a hot summer day. These pops are all that and more! With only three ingredients, it's easy to whip up a batch.

serves 8

Ingredients

| 8 ounces semi-sweet chocolate | ⅔ cup cream plus ¾ cup cream, divided | 1 Tbsp. butter |

Directions

In a medium-sized saucepan, warm ⅔ cup cream and 1 tablespoon butter over medium-low heat.

Cook until butter melts and small bubbles form around the outside edge of the cream. Remove from the heat and add the chocolate. Let it sit for 1 minute before stirring until smooth.

Set in the fridge for 30-45 minutes or until cool. Once cool, add ¾ cup cream and beat until smooth. Pour into molds and place in the freezer for 4-6 hours or overnight.

To remove the cream pop from the mold, run the bottom of the mold under warm water for 15 seconds making sure the water doesn't touch the top of the mold. Pull on the handle to see if the pop will slide out. If it doesn't move, run the water over it again. Continue until the pop slides out.

mini chocolate chip muffins

If you're planning a large meal, a small dessert can be the best ending. These mini muffins are sweet and chocolatey enough to crown any get together and they're a snap to make and to make look good.

makes 32 mini muffins

Muffins

¼ cup milk chocolate chips	1 tsp. vanilla	½ cup brown sugar
¼ cup butter	1 cup flour	¼ cup mini chocolate chips
1 Tbsp. cocoa powder	½ tsp. baking soda	
1 egg	A pinch of salt	

Glaze

1 Tbsp. butter	½ cup powdered sugar	extra mini chocolate chips for garnish, if desired
¼ cup chocolate hazelnut spread	1 Tbsp. water	

Directions

Preheat the oven to 325 degrees. Spray a mini muffin pan with nonstick cooking spray and set aside.

In a small saucepan, melt the chocolate chips and butter together. Stir in the cocoa powder, egg and vanilla and set aside. In a medium-sized mixing bowl stir together the flour, baking soda, salt and brown sugar. Add the chocolate mixture and stir well. Stir in the mini chocolate chips and spoon the batter into the prepared pan filling the cups about halfway full. Bake for 8-10 minutes or until a toothpick inserted in the center comes out clean. When the muffins are done, run a knife around the edges and transfer the muffins to a wire rack to cool.

For the glaze: In a small saucepan, melt the butter. Add the hazelnut spread, powdered sugar, and water and beat by hand until smooth. Immediately, dip the top of a muffin into the glaze. Twist as you're pulling the muffin out to decrease the drips. Sprinkle with additional mini chocolate chips if desired and serve.

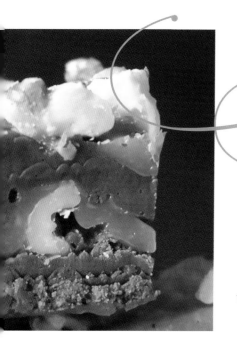

Candy

Candy—a chocolate lover's go-to for a chocolate fix. The wonderful thing about making your own candy is that you can immerse yourself in the experience—literally. More often than not, I dip my candy by hand. It's like a spa treatment and productive afternoon all rolled into one. You can, of course, use a dipping fork or toothpicks instead of covering yourself in chocolate. But I believe everyone should try it at least once in their lives. Think about it, how many times, since you graduated from kindergarten, have you stuck your clean hands into something and let your inner child have fun? For most of us, the opportunities are too far and few between.

103   daddy treats (peanut butter cups)

104   truffle pops

107   grandma lucy's nut balls

108   cookie dough dreams

111   fondant

114   peppermint discs

117   turtle fudge

daddy treats
(peanut butter cups)

A long time ago, when my children were little and still had toothless grins, my oldest son noticed his dad ate a lot of peanut butter treats found in an orange wrapper. When he wanted one, he would ask for a "Daddy Treat." Though the years have sped by, in our home, peanut butter cups have retained the distinction as daddy's treats.

makes 24 peanut butter cups

Ingredients

1½ cup milk chocolate chips

1½ Tbsp. shortening

2 large graham crackers

¼ cup creamy peanut butter

¼ cup butter at room temperature

½ cup powdered sugar

Directions

Place 24 mini muffin cup liners in the recesses of a muffin pan and set aside.

In a small saucepan, melt the chocolate chips and shortening over low heat stirring often. Once the chocolate is smooth, set it aside.

Crush the graham crackers and place in a medium-sized mixing bowl. Add the peanut butter, butter, and powdered sugar. Beat until it turns into a paste.

Place the chocolate mixture in a plastic zip top bag. Snip off a small portion of one corner. Squeeze a small portion of chocolate into the bottom of each cup. Fill a second bag with the peanut butter paste, snip the corner, and fill the muffin liners ⅔ of the way full. Try to keep the peanut butter in the center of the cup so the chocolate can fill in on the sides. Use the remaining chocolate to cover the peanut butter paste. Gently tap the pan on the counter a couple times to get the chocolate to settle evenly in the cups. Set aside for 1-3 hours to set. If needed place the pan in the fridge for 20 minutes.

truffle pops

The perfect party favor, these Truffle Pops will impress guests of all ages. You can tie them to the top of a gift with ribbon, create a stunning gift basket, or hand them out one at a time to dear friends. For a variation, try adding a ½ teaspoon of mint, almond, or orange flavoring when you add the vanilla.

makes 36 pops

Ingredients

2 cups of chocolate chips, milk or semi-sweet will work

1 (14-oz.) can sweetened condensed milk

1 tsp. vanilla

12 ounces of dipping chocolate

sprinkles or additional

chocolate for garnish

36 sucker sticks

36 mini treat bags

tape or ribbon

Directions

Prepare a 5½ × 7½-inch pan by lining it with aluminum foil. Set aside.

In a medium-sized saucepan, melt the chocolate chips and sweetened condensed milk. Stir occasionally and remove from heat once the mixture is smooth. Add the vanilla and mix well. Pour the chocolate into the prepared pan and place in the refrigerator making sure the pan is level. Chill for 2–4 hours.

When the truffle center is set, lift the chocolate out using the aluminum foil. Peel away the foil and, using a long knife, cut the chocolate into 36 pieces. Insert a sucker stick into each piece and stand it on a wax paper lined plate or cookie sheet. Place the suckers in the fridge while you melt the dipping chocolate. Lay a piece of wax paper on the work surface. Holding the sucker stick, dip each truffle in the chocolate. Tap the sucker stick against the edge of the pan to remove the excess chocolate and then carefully lay the sucker on the sheet of wax paper. Repeat with each sucker. If adding sprinkles or nuts, do so before the chocolate sets. If garnishing with additional chocolate, you can do so after the suckers harden. Once the chocolate has cooled and set, you can wrap the suckers using tape or ribbon to close off the bags.

grandma lucy's nut balls

These cream and nut balls were a special treat at Christmas time. When we arrived at my grandparents', I would eagerly scan for the candy dish. I've tweaked the recipe just a bit, but I don't think Grandma would mind.

makes 25
Ingredients

½ pound of butter at room temperature	2 cups powdered sugar	16 ounces of chocolate for dipping
¼ cup sweetened condensed milk	¼ tsp. salt	2 cups roasted and chopped almonds
	1 tsp. clear vanilla	

Directions

Cover a cookie sheet with wax paper and set aside.

In a medium-sized mixing bowl, beat the butter until light and fluffy. Add the sweetened condensed milk, powdered sugar, salt and vanilla and beat until mixture lightens in color—about 1 minute. Spoon by tablespoonful onto prepared cookie sheet. You should get 25 dollops or so. Place the cookie sheet in the freezer for 1-3 hours or until set. Melt the chocolate in a double broiler. Remove the creams from the freezer and immediately dip in melted chocolate and roll in nuts. Place on a piece of wax paper to set!

Variation: Add ½ teaspoon rum flavoring.

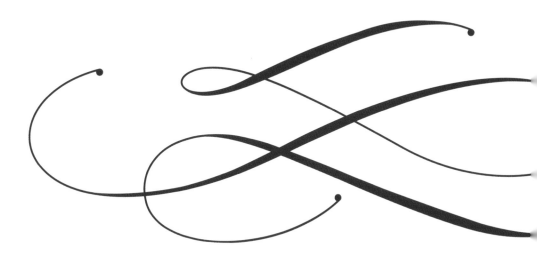

cookie dough dreams

These sweet, chocolate-covered cookie dough drops will remind you of snitching cookie dough from the bowl. However, the recipe is void of eggs so you've no need to worry about getting sick—unless you eat too many.

makes 36

Ingredients

¾ cup butter at room temperature

⅓ cup sugar

¾ cup brown sugar

½ tsp. coconut flavoring

¼ tsp. salt

3 Tbsp. milk

2 cups flour

16 ounces chocolate

Directions

Cover a cookie sheet with freezer paper and set aside.

In a medium-sized mixing bowl, beat the butter until light and fluffy. Add the sugar, brown sugar, coconut flavoring, salt, and milk and mix well. Finally, add the flour and beat until well combined.

Make tablespoon-sized balls of dough and place on the cookie sheet. You don't have to leave space between the balls of dough as if you were cooking them. Place the cookie sheet in the freezer while you melt the chocolate.

Once the chocolate is ready and the dough has set for a half hour, dip each ball in the chocolate and place on a sheet of wax paper to set. Once set, store in the refrigerator in a covered container or zip-top bag.

fondant

Growing up, the day after Thanksgiving was Chocolate Day. For weeks beforehand, the women in my family would prepare fondant, caramels, and fudges; they'd purchase large, delicious smelling, bricks of chocolate and shopping bags full of nuts. We'd pull out the candy cups, boxes, and tins used for storage and gift-giving. Then, on the designated day, we'd dip between 75 and 100 pounds of chocolate, nut clusters, caramels, cherries, fudges, and whatever else wasn't nailed down. This is our fondant recipe. I hope you enjoy it!

makes 60 candy centers

Ingredients

3 cups sugar

1 cup heavy cream

½ cup milk

⅓ tsp. cream of tartar

1 Tbsp. white corn syrup

1 tsp. flavoring, your choice

16 ounces of dipping chocolate

food coloring

butter, at room temperature, for greasing platter

Directions

Stir together all the ingredients in a large saucepan. The mixture will boil up to double in size so plan for expansion. Turn the burner on to medium heat. Place the pan on the burner and insert a candy thermometer clipping it to the side of the pan so it doesn't move around. Remove all wooden spoons or mixing utensils and cook until the mixture comes to 223-224 degrees on the candy thermometer. DO NOT stir the fondant as it cooks as this will cause it to "sugar" and be grainy instead of smooth. While the fondant comes to temperature, spread butter over the bottom and up the sides of a large serving platter. We used the same platter we served the turkey on for Thanksgiving. When the fondant reaches the right temperature, you can pour it onto the buttered platter and let it cool until the edges are set or you pull in an edge with a fork and it drags the fondant making a V. Add the flavoring and food coloring and, using a sturdy fork, beat the fondant by tipping one edge up and scraping under the fondant with the fork, pulling it back up

toward the top of the platter. Continue until the fondant becomes cloudy and hard to beat. Transfer the fondant to a plastic bag or container with a lid. Can store in the fridge for 2 weeks. To prepare fondant for dipping, sprinkle a light layer of powdered sugar on your work surface. You can work the whole batch of fondant or break it into smaller, more manageable sections if needed. Allow the fondant to sit at room temper for 10-15 minutes before working. Roll the fondant into a 1-inch wide tube as if you were working with play dough. Cut off ½-inch sections and roll them into balls. They are now ready for dipping.

NOTE: If the fondant "sugars" you can recook it. Simply place the fondant in a large saucepan, add 1¼ cups water and 1 tablespoon of corn syrup. You may stir the mixture until the fondant dissolves in the water, then follow the same instructions above, adding the flavoring again. Recooking will increase the size of the batch so you'll need more chocolate for dipping.

Instructions for dipping chocolates by hand

If you're right handed, place the prepared fondant balls on the left of your work station. Directly in front of you will be your clean granite slab. Above the slab will be your melted chocolate. And on your right will be a cookie sheet covered in waxed paper.

Scoop up a handful of chocolate and let half of it drip back into the pan. Now, move so you are positioned to work over the granite. You'll work from left to right. Use your left hand to pick up a fondant ball and drop it into your right hand. Gently roll the ball to cover it with chocolate. Wipe the excess chocolate off the side of your hand, scraping it in an arch across the granite. Move over the wax paper and drop the ball onto the tray.

At this point, you can make designs with the chocolate as you gain more experience. Zig-zags, letters, circles, hearts, etc. are all popular ways to differentiate between the flavors of fondants. You can also sprinkle them with different colored sprinkles, nuts, or chocolate shavings.

Once the tray is full, you'll need a helper to move the tray to a cool room. The room should not feel cold, about 72 degrees is fine, and free from drafts. Drafts will cause the chocolates to "bloom" or develop the white streaks you sometimes see. Allow the chocolates to set before placing them in candy cups and boxing.

peppermint discs

Dark chocolate is the traditional covering for peppermint discs. Because the peppermint is a strong flavor, it needs the stronger chocolate to balance it out.

makes 20

Ingredients

2 cups powdered sugar

1½ Tbsp. butter at room temperature

2 Tbsp. cream

2 tsp. peppermint flavoring

10 ounces dark chocolate

1 Tbsp. shortening

Directions

Place the powdered sugar, butter, cream, and peppermint flavoring in a medium-sized mixing bowl or the bowl of a stand mixer. Beat together until the mixture forms a paste. This can take up to 5 minutes. When done, shape the mixture into a 1-inch round tube.

Wrap the tube in plastic wrap and place in the refrigerator for 1 hour. Once set, cut the tube into ¼-inch discs and place them on a cookie sheet lined with wax paper. Place the cookie sheet in the freezer while you melt the chocolate and shortening together in a medium-sized saucepan over medium-low heat.

Once the chocolate is smooth, remove 2-3 discs from the freezer and dip them in the chocolate. Set them on a sheet of wax paper and allow to set. Repeat with remaining discs.

turtle fudge

The basic fudge recipe is a wonderful base for mix-ins. In this recipe, I've added caramel and nuts. However, you could use chopped fruit, peanut butter cups, bite-sized candy, pretzels, or even potato chips. Or, if you're in the mood for plain fudge, leave the mix-ins out and indulge in the smooth chocolate.

makes 25 squares

Ingredients

1 bag (10-oz.) caramels, unwrapped	4 ounces (16) marshmallows	1 (14-oz.) can sweetened condensed milk
2 Tbsp. cream	3 cups milk chocolate chips	1 cup nuts (optional)

Directions

Line a 9 × 9-inch pan with aluminum foil. Set aside. In a small saucepan, melt the caramels and cream together over medium-low heat stirring occasionally. After you've started the caramels, you can start the fudge. You want them to be ready at the same time so you'll have to watch both pans.

Break the marshmallows in half and place them in a large saucepan, add the sweetened condensed milk and melt over medium-low heat until marshmallows start to melt. Stir occasionally. Once the marshmallows start to melt, add the chocolate chips. When the chocolate and caramels have melted completely, remove the pans from the burners.

Pour half the fudge into the pan, spreading it to the edges. Drizzle with half the caramel and half the nuts if desired. Be careful not to let the caramel touch the aluminum foil as it will stick making it difficult to get the fudge out of the pan. Repeat the layers, pressing the nuts into the top of the fudge. Refrigerate for 2 hours. If the caramel gets too hard in the fridge, allow the pan to set at room temperature for 10–15 minutes before cutting.

Sauces, Fillings, and Frostings

Exchanging one type of frosting for another can switch up a recipe enough that it can seem brand new. With that in mind, I've provided the recipes for several of my go-to toppings. They are all wonderful and have been used over and over again throughout the years. I'm sure they'll become staples in your recipe collection as well.

180   chocolate glaze

180   marshmallow filling

181   peanut butter frosting

181   one-bag chocolate ganache

182   chocolate mousse

184   chocolate frosting

184   fudge frosting

185   white chocolate drizzle

185   fudge sauce

chocolate glaze

This glaze is delicious on the Chocolate Zucchini Bundt Cake (page 40) or any other cake really.

makes enough to cover 1 cake

Ingredients

3 ounces semi-sweet chocolate

2 Tbsp. butter

2 Tbsp. cream

1 Tbsp. corn syrup

Directions

Chop the chocolate into dime-sized pieces. Place chocolate in a small saucepan and add the butter, cream, and corn syrup. Melt over medium-low heat, stirring constantly until the mixture is smooth. Allow to cool for 5 minutes before drizzling over cake.

marshmallow filling

This is a great recipe for filling everything from Chocolate Crêpes (page 94) to Snowball Brownies (page 14). It's sweet and a little goes a long way.

Ingredients

2 tsp. hot water

¼ tsp. salt

1 (7-oz.) jar of marshmallow cream

½ cup shortening

½ cup powdered sugar

1 tsp. clear vanilla

Directions

Place the hot water and salt in a small bowl and stir until the salt dissolves. Set aside.

In a medium-sized mixing bowl, combine the marshmallow cream, shortening, powdered sugar, and vanilla. The mixture wills stick to the beaters at first, just keep going, beating together for a full 2 minutes. While the beaters are still on, add 1 teaspoon of the saltwater. Mix it in. If the marshmallow filling is still too stiff, add another ¼ of a teaspoon of saltwater. Continue adding saltwater until the filling reaches the desired consistency. Use immediately.

peanut butter frosting

makes enough to frost one batch of brownies

Ingredients

2 Tbsp. creamy peanut butter | 1 tsp. vanilla | ¼ tsp. salt
2 Tbsp. milk | 2 cups powdered sugar

Directions

Melt the peanut butter and milk in a small saucepan over low heat. Once smooth, remove from heat and add vanilla, powdered sugar, and salt. Spread over brownies, cake, or cookies. Refrigerate any leftover frosting for up to 4 days in a covered container.

one-bag chocolate ganache

A quick and delicious chocolate ganache made using one bag of chocolate chips. While you can certainly use generic chocolate, I find the best results come from Ghiradelli semi-sweet premium baking chips.

Ingredients

1 bag (12-oz.) semi-sweet chocolate chips. | ⅓ cup heavy cream | 1 Tbsp. butter

Directions

In a medium saucepan, over low heat, melt the chocolate chips, cream, and butter together stirring occasionally. Once all the lumps are gone, remove the pan from the heat and use immediately.

chocolate mousse

The recipe says "serves 4" but I don't usually serve the mousse alone. Instead, I use it to fill cakes and cupcakes. It can also be served as pictured here, layered with crushed cookie crumbs.

serves 4

Ingredients

8 ounces milk chocolate	1 Tbsp. butter
½ cup cream, divided	

Directions

In a medium-sized saucepan, melt the chocolate chips, 2 Tbsp. of the cream, and the butter. Stir occasionally and remove from the heat as soon as the mixture is smooth. Transfer to a mixing bowl and place in the refrigerator for 30-45 minutes. Remove the cooled mixture from the refrigerator and stir it 8-12 times to loosen it up. Add 2 tablespoons of cream and mix well. Add the rest of the cream and whip until light. Do not over mix or the mousse will be lumpy. Store, covered, in the refrigerator.

chocolate frosting

This is a thick frosting that sets up quickly and will hold its shape. You can use milk or semi-sweet chocolate chips depending on your preference.

makes enough to frost one batch of brownies

Ingredients

1 cup chocolate chips	½ tsp. salt	¼ cup milk
¼ cup cream	2 Tbsp. cocoa powder	1 tsp. vanilla
3½ cups powdered sugar		

Directions

Melt the chocolate chips and cream together over medium-low heat, stirring frequently. Once melted, allow to cool for 5-10 minutes. In a medium-sized mixing bowl, combine the chocolate mixture, powdered sugar, salt, cocoa powder, milk, and vanilla. Beat until well combined scraping down the sides of the bowl. Use immediately.

fudge frosting

This is my Grandma Joyce's frosting recipe. It can be used on cakes, cupcakes, brownies, or eaten by the spoonful. It's also delicious frozen. Don't ask me how I know that . . .

makes enough to frost one batch of brownies

Ingredients

½ cup butter, melted	1 tsp. vanilla	⅔ cup whipping cream
½ cup cocoa powder	½ tsp. salt	6-8 cups powdered sugar, divided

Directions

Mix together the butter, cocoa powder, vanilla, and salt. Add the whipping cream and 4 cups of powdered sugar. Continue to add powdered sugar one cup at a time until you reach your desired consistency. You may not use all 8 cups of powdered sugar.

white chocolate drizzle

White chocolate is not considered real chocolate because it doesn't contain cacao, hence the white color. It does contain cacao butter, which comes from the cacao bean, making it a nice addition to a chocolate dish. Because it doesn't have cacao, it will not melt well with milk products. Instead, use other types of fat like cooking oil or shortening to thing the white chocolate when melting.

makes enough to drizzle over 1 cake

Ingredients

1¼ cup white chocolate chips | 1 tablespoon shortening

Directions

In a small saucepan over low heat, melt the white chocolate chips and the shortening together stirring often. When the mixture is smooth, you can use a zip-top bag with the corner cut off to drizzle the sauce over your cake, cookies, or brownies.

fudge sauce

For a quick ice cream or cake topping, try this delicious fudge sauce.

Ingredients

1 (14-oz.) can sweetened condensed milk | 1½ cups chocolate chips (milk or semi-sweet) | ½ cup butter
1 teaspoon vanilla

Directions

In a medium saucepan over low heat, melt the sweetened condensed milk, chocolate chips and butter until smooth. Add the vanilla and stir well. Serve immediately or allow to cool.

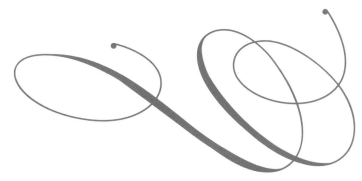

Index

B

blueberry and white chocolate
  cookies 66

brownie bottom cheesecake 43

C

chocolate almond cake 39

chocolate almond press cookies 77

chocolate and peanut butter cookies 73

chocolate cheesecake 44

chocolate chunk cookies 57

chocolate cookie pie 51

chocolate crêpes 94

chocolate dream pie 35

chocolate frosting 124

chocolate fudge cookies 74

chocolate glaze 120

chocolate heaven 52

chocolate info 1

chocolate mousse 122

chocolate pudding 90

chocolate summer cake 36

chocolate tart 89

chocolate twists 93

chocolate zucchini bundt cake 40

coconut and chocolate cookies 65

cookie dough brownies 18

cookie dough dreams 108

cream pops 97

D

daddy treats (peanut butter cups)   103

dark chocolate cookies   69

deep, dark, blue moon pie   48

F

fondant   111

fudge frosting   124

fudge sauce   125

fudgety-fudge brownies   10

G

grandma joyce's 24-hour brownies   22

grandma lucy's nut balls   107

M

marshmallow filling   120

mini chocolate chip muffins   98

mint brownies   25

mint chocolate cookies   61

mom's best fudge cake   47

N

nothin' but chocolate gooey bars   13

O

oatmeal pan cookies   70

one-bag chocolate ganache   121

orange chocolate cake   32

P

peanut butter & chocolate tart   85

peanut butter frosting   121

pecan and chocolate cookie bars   17

peppermint discs   114

pumpkin cheesecake & chocolate swirl
    brownies   29

R

rolayne's chocolate chip cookies   62

S

simple chocolate ice cream   81

s'mores ice cream   82

snowball brownies   14

striped brownies   26

T

the king of brownies   21

toffee bottom fudge tart   86

truffle pops   104

turtle fudge   117

W

white chocolate drizzle   125

world's most addictive cookie   58

Cooking Measurement Equivalents

Cups	Tablespoons	Fluid Ounces
⅛ cup	2 Tbsp.	1 fl. oz.
¼ cup	4 Tbsp.	2 fl. oz.
⅓ cup	5 Tbsp. + 1 tsp.	
½ cup	8 Tbsp.	4 fl. oz.
⅔ cup	10 Tbsp. + 2 tsp.	
¾ cup	12 Tbsp.	6 fl. oz.
1 cup	16 Tbsp.	8 fl. oz.

Cups	Fluid Ounces	Pints/Quarts/Gallons
1 cup	8 fl. oz.	½ pint
2 cups	16 fl. oz.	1 pint = ½ quart
3 cups	24 fl. oz.	1½ pints
4 cups	32 fl. oz.	2 pints = 1 quart
8 cups	64 fl. oz.	2 quarts = ½ gallon
16 cups	128 fl. oz.	4 quarts = 1 gallon

Other Helpful Equivalents

1 Tbsp.	3 tsp.
8 oz.	½ lb.
16 oz.	1 lb.

Metric Measurement Equivalents

Approximate Weight Equivalents

Ounces	Pounds	Grams
4 oz.	¼ lb.	113 g
5 oz.		142 g
6 oz.		170 g
8 oz.	½ lb.	227 g
9 oz.		255 g
12 oz.	¾ lb.	340 g
16 oz.	1 lb.	454 g

Approximate Volume Equivalents

Cups	US Fluid Ounces	Milliliters
⅛ cup	1 fl. oz.	30 ml
¼ cup	2 fl. oz.	59 ml
½ cup	4 fl. oz.	118 ml
¾ cup	6 fl. oz.	177 ml
1 cup	8 fl. oz.	237 ml

Other Helpful Equivalents

½ tsp.	2½ ml
1 tsp.	5 ml
1 Tbsp.	15 ml

About the Author

Christina Dymock is the author of *The Hungry Family Slow Cooker Cookbook*, *The Bacon Lover's Cookbook*, *One Dirty Bowl: Fast Baking, Faster Cleanup*, and several other cookbooks. She has also written for *Deseret News* and been interviewed for *Parents Magazine* and other national publications. Christina's fiction and short stories have been published in *Woman's World Magazine* and seven *Chicken Soup for the Soul* books, and you can find her clean romances under the pen name Lucy McConnell.

To contact Christina, visit her blog at CHRISTINADYMOCK.WORDPRESS.COM

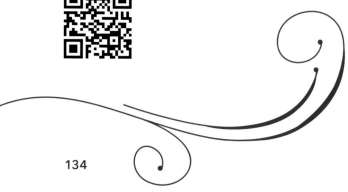